SANCTIFICATION

BY JASON HENDERSON

**This and other publications
are available <u>FREE</u> upon request
by contacting:**

Market Street Fellowship
981 W. Market Street   Akron, Ohio 44311
email: MSFPrinting@gmail.com
phone: 330-419-1527
v.2

*This publication was originally a series of spoken messages given at Market Street Fellowship in March of 2009. The reader is asked to bear in mind that the **spoken form** is retained throughout this publication.*

Contents

I	Separation	7
II	The Process of Sanctification	15
III	The Division of the Cross	23
IV	Christ the Door	30
V	Living in the Earth	38
VI	The Journey	44
VII	The Great Divide	53
VIII	Seek Those Things Which Are Above	65
IX	Crossing the Jordan	70

Chapter I
Separation

Ephesians 5:25 *Husbands, love your wives, even as Christ also loved the church and gave Himself up on its behalf, 26 that He might <u>sanctify it</u>, cleansing it by the washing of the water in the Word.*

John 17:17 *<u>Sanctify them in Your Truth</u>; Your Word is Truth. 18 As You have sent Me into the world, I also have sent them into the world, 19 and <u>I sanctify Myself for them, that they also may be sanctified in Truth</u>.*

Acts 20:32 *And now, brothers, I commend you to God and to the Word of His grace, which is able to build up and to give you inheritance <u>among all those being sanctified.</u>*

Acts 26:14 *And all of us falling to the ground, I heard a voice speaking to me, and saying in the*

Hebrew dialect, Saul, Saul why do you persecute Me? It is hard for you to kick against the prods. 15 And I said, Who are you, Sir? And He said, I am Jesus whom you persecute; 16 but rise up and stand on your feet, for it is for this reason I appeared to you, to appoint you a servant and a witness both of what you saw, and in what I shall appear to you, 17 having delivered you from the people and the nations, to whom I now send you, 18 to open their eyes, and to turn them from darkness to light, and from the authority of Satan to God, in order that they may receive remission of sins, <u>and an inheritance among those being sanctified by faith in Me</u>.

1Peter 1:3 *Blessed be the God and Father of our Lord Jesus Christ, He according to His great mercy having regenerated us to a living hope (lit. expectation) through the resurrection of Jesus Christ from the dead, 4 to an inheritance incorruptible and undefiled and unfading, having been kept in Heaven for you 5 the ones in the power of God being guarded through faith to a salvation ready to be revealed in the last time.*

2Thessalonians 2:13 *But we ought to thank God always concerning you, brothers, beloved by the Lord, because God chose you from the beginning <u>to salvation in sanctification of the Spirit and faith in the truth</u>, 14 to which He called you through our gospel, to obtain the glory of our Lord Jesus Christ.*

What is sanctification? It is definitely a common word in the body of Christ, but one that is also very misunderstood. Sanctification is not a process of becoming more like Christ through discipline, effort, or abstaining from so-called unchristian things. It does not involve dedicating yourself to the Lord or to the church. In fact, sanctification is not something that we do. Nor is it something that we avoid doing.

It does, in fact, involve being conformed to the image of Christ. That much is true. Sanctification is a process whereby we are transformed, changed, conformed to the indwelling life of Christ. Most theological textbooks will have this much correct. But it's the *process* itself that so many are confused about. It's **the nature of the process, the way that this happens, the question of HOW** - that is where we are so much in the dark.

Sanctification has to do with separation. Sometimes the word is simply defined as a "setting apart." Consecration is a word that means very close to the same thing. But again, what do we understand about this separation? What are we separated from? How does that separation take place? Paul says in Ephesians 5:25 that we are sanctified by the washing of the water of the word. In another of the verses we read, Paul said that we are sanctified by the Spirit through faith in the truth. These are describing the exact same thing. But before we get into that, let's first look at the question of what we are separated from.

The Nature of the Fall

T. Austin-Sparks writes this: "With the Fall, an entangling with another nature and order took place. It became organic, therefore constitutional." That is a very brief, but accurate summary. We cannot understand sanctification until we understand what it is that we need to be separated from. As a race, we have fallen. Fallen *from* something, indeed. Fallen from the glory of God. Fallen from purpose. **But also fallen INTO something.** Fallen into an entanglement with a nature and order that maintains deep control over our soul, that has complete jurisdiction over our being. It is impossible to accurately depict the nature of this entanglement. Hearing about it does nothing; you have to see it.

Man has always been a soul. That soul was breathed into our earthen vessel on the day he was created. Genesis says that God "blew His breath into man's nostrils and man became a living soul." That soul, as you well know, was created to be the habitation for the living God, the perfect and only environment for the glory of God to indwell. If you can bear the weakness of this analogy, that soul was a little bit like a sponge, that had in itself the capacity to absorb into itself, bear in itself, hold and carry pure, clean water. And when that sponge fell from glory, it didn't just fall **out** of a bucket of water. It fell **into** a swamp of sewage and sickness that saturated every crevice and pore. That is something of the nature of man's fall. That is a picture of man's entanglement with all that is contrary to God.

Jesus once said, "You are those that justify yourselves before men, but the things that are highly esteemed in the eyes of man are detestable in the sight of God" (Luke 16:15). That word "detestable" has always frightened me. It's such a strong word, but not too strong when the Light of His life shows us what we are.

Despite our objections to the contrary and our utter blindness to the reality, our soul is born twisted and knotted up in a nature and order that now constrains all that we think, want, and do. It is a nature and order that is without God, and therefore without glory. It is the profound and overpowering relationship that Paul the apostle calls "slavery to sin." All of this is the effect of the lie that we believed in the garden.

Sanctification has to do with the solution, the reversing of this situation. First of all it has to do with the objective fact of what was accomplished at the cross. In the cross of Jesus Christ the first was separated from the second, death was separated from life, Adam was separated from Christ. Having gone into the sickness and blackness of fallen humanity, having born its guilt and shame before God, having taken it out of God's sight, out of God's camp, like the scapegoat of old, Jesus was lifted up out from the earth. It's like He was projected out of the earth, vomited up from the belly of the earth because He was too righteous to be held, too perfect to remain there. He needed to die there, but He could not remain there. The earth could not hold Him. Having put away sin from the sight of God, Christ had no more business with that realm and order and kind.

And so He left. He separated Himself from that realm and nature and order. This is the glory of the ascension. He ascended so that He might fill all things. He ascended bringing many sons to glory. He ascended so that He would forever be separated from the first man and first creation, **and so that WE could be separated in Him**.

This is what was on the mind of the Lord Jesus the night before He went to the cross. This is what He spoke to His Father about in the presence of His disciples. "Father, I desire that those who you have given me be with me where I am." And then he said, "For this reason I sanctify Myself, that they also may be sanctified in me." For this reason I am separated from that death, that they might be separated in Me. For this reason I have come up from among the dead, that I might be to them the Resurrection and the Life. For this reason I have put away the first, that I may appear to them in the second, without reference to sin, unto salvation.

Can you see the nature of sanctification here? In a moment I will talk about the process of sanctification, but the process is only the soul's possession and appropriation of this objective reality. The nature of sanctification has to do with *separation*. **It has to do with leaving something so far behind that it is forgotten and meaningless.** Indeed, the former things no longer even come to mind. They are separated as far as the east is from the west.

Christ, before He became a man, was already separated from the fallen nature and order of man. But He came to make a door. He made a door through His death. His death is offered to us as our door, and this death becomes our death too. If we will walk into that death and embrace all that that death means, then we will find Jacob's ladder on the other side. A ladder that reaches into the heavens, that takes us in Him to where He is. "I am in the Father, you are in Me, I am in you."

The Soul's Disentanglement

The Lord Jesus Christ cut between these realms and realities with a sharp sword and the division will never heal. It is permanent and immovable. And now, all that God has and God wants and God has relationship with, is on the side that is represented by Christ. I realize that God has relationship with believers who still have earthen bodies, but those bodies do not define the location and habitation and inheritance of the soul. For you and I, for us RIGHT NOW, we are raised up and seated with Christ in the heavens. It makes no difference where our bodies are. It is the home of the soul that is in view. We have been sanctified as a matter of fact, as a matter of God's perspective. **And yet there remains the inward disentanglement with the order and nature that God has disassociated with.**

We are in Christ. There is no question about that. **But we are in Christ as those who, by nature, are part of what God has forsaken.** We are in Christ, we are in heaven, but we are there as those who begin our journey exclusively conscious of the WRONG REALM. There is the fact of our being translated out of the kingdom of darkness and into the kingdom of the Son of God's love. **And then there is the inward separation, the soul's disentanglement, with what God has abandoned.** There is the fact of having left Egypt, and then there is the experience of Egypt leaving our hearts. There is the fact of Ishmael being sent out of Abraham's sight, and then there is the experience of coming to know Isaac as the only son.

The fact of what God has done is finished and cannot be contended with. God has taken the sponge soaked with mud and permanently deposited it into an ocean of pure living water. It is there forever and will never be anywhere else. But still there is the filth and sludge that has saturated every pore. That mud is not your bad habits or your bad language or your bad behavior. That mud is what you have called your life. That mud is everything that you have ever been and known and thought and wanted. That mud is both what you desired and why you desired it. It is you, the self-life that your soul has always called "me." That mud is the residue of a nature and order that you associate with yourself. And so there needs to be something drastic done about this. There needs to be a thorough purging and erasing and mortifying of all that is not water in this ocean of living water. That brings us to the question of how this works.

Chapter II
The Process of Sanctification

What is the process of sanctification? What is the method? What kind of soap could actually cleanse the human conscience? That is what Hebrews calls this process – the cleansing of the conscience. Not simply resolving a guilty conscience, but actually permanently altering what you are conscious of. Removing from you your consciousness of what lies behind the cross. Cleansing your conscience so that it corresponds to what God sees and knows. So what has the power to expunge an entire false life and reality from our heart? Only one thing - **only the living Word of God. Only the Truth. It is truth that washes us from all that is a lie. It is truth that removes from us what has no place in God.**

The Spirit of Truth

But what is Truth? Pontius Pilate asked that question two thousand years ago. Jesus didn't answer him because the answer is not found in words. Jesus didn't answer Pilate because Pilate was looking at Truth and couldn't see it, and no words were going to solve that problem. We need to settle this issue in our hearts. Truth can be described by words. Truth can be described by the pages of your Bible, but words cannot contain the truth. Making application of words to *your* life is powerless and pointless. True words will never sanctify your soul.

Truth is the soul's apprehension of Christ our life. Truth is the person and place and life and reality of Christ known by the Spirit. Truth has to do with inwardly possessing the finished work of Christ by revelation. Truth involves the reality of where Christ lives, what Christ is, how Christ sees. If we will only let the Spirit of God show us *this* truth, then we will occupy and abide in Christ. We will be set apart, separated unto, sanctified in the Truth. "Father, sanctify them in the Truth. Your Word is Truth. For this reason I sanctify myself, that they also may be sanctified in the Truth."

Sanctification is where the Spirit of Truth guides us into all truth, and separates us from everything else. Do you know that for you who are born again, everything other than the Truth is a lie? Have you faced that yet? Have you faced the fact that once you are born of the truth, ignorance of the truth is an acceptance of and an agreement with the lie? People have said to me before, "What's the big deal about Christians not knowing the Truth? We're all going to heaven one day anyway, and I'm sure we'll figure it out then." Besides the obvious problems with theology there, the question overlooks a very serious point. **To refuse the Truth is to prefer the Lie. Ignorance is not bliss; ignorance is death.**

Ignorance is contrariness to the person and purpose of God. Ignorance for a Christian is a love-affair with the Lie. If we will not grow up in the truth, ignorance is just another face of rebellion. "No thank you, God, I'll take my inheritance here on the other side of the Jordan." God replies, "There is no inheritance there, except for the one in your imagination that is established in opposition to Me."

That is why we must follow the Lord fully like Joshua and Caleb. We must follow the Lord with all of our heart and soul and mind and strength, and let Him show us what is real, let Him show us the Land. You cannot stop along the way. I mean, of course you CAN, but to stop along the way is to cling to something that is not even real. It is to prefer ignorance over Truth. To reject reality in favor of a deadly fantasy.

Like Abraham so long ago, the Spirit of truth leads us into a land that must be revealed. "Abraham, leave your country, kindred, and father's house, and go unto a land that I WILL SHOW YOU." Sanctification is where the Spirit of Truth escorts us into a heavenly land, and all that we have called country, kindred, and father's house is forgotten and forsaken. Everything that was part of what we were, where we were, and that to which we belonged. None of it had anything to do with Abraham's inheritance. It wasn't true of him any longer, and all of it had to be washed away from his soul in order for him to see and receive the inheritance.

Abraham could possess nothing through a natural inheritance. He could possess nothing by natural effort or natural vision or natural association. He tried to bring his father. He tried to bring his relative, Lot. He tried to create the seed of promise through Ishmael, but God would not let Abraham inherit something of the earth. God had set him apart for a heavenly inheritance.

When Abraham first arrived at the land there was nothing. There were arguments with locals and a famine that sent him fleeing to Egypt. There was nothing in that land for him according to *sight*. With his natural eyes there was nothing there for him to possess. We hear the Lord's call to him again and again – "Lift up your eyes, Abraham, and look. Lift up your eyes. You will not, indeed you cannot, see My inheritance if your eyes are looking down here. It is a heavenly land. It is a heavenly inheritance. You cannot inherit My promise unless you are set apart from all that was previous. You will not experience My inheritance until you are separated unto it, until you are sanctified by faith."

You can see this reality in the following story.

> ***Genesis 13:5*** *And Lot, who went with Abram, also had flocks and herds and tents. 6 And the land was not able to bear them, that they might live together. For their substance was great, <u>so that they could not live together</u>. 7 And there was strife between the herdsmen of Abram's cattle and the herdsmen of Lot's cattle. And the Canaanite and the Perizzite lived then in the land. 8 And Abram said to Lot, Let there be no strife, I pray you, between me and you, and between my herdsmen and your herdsmen; for we are men, brothers. 9 Is not the whole land before you? I pray you, <u>separate yourself from me</u>. If you go to*

the left, then I will go to the right. Or if you go to the right, then I will go to the left. 10 And Lot lifted up his eyes and saw all the circuit of Jordan, that it was all well watered (before Jehovah destroyed Sodom and Gomorrah,) like the garden of Jehovah, like the land of Egypt as you come to Zoar. 11 And Lot chose all the circuit of Jordan for himself. And Lot journeyed east; and they separated themselves from one another. 12 Abram lived in the land of Canaan, and Lot lived in the cities of the circuit and pitched his tent toward Sodom. 13 But the men of Sodom were wicked and sinners before Jehovah, exceedingly so. 14 <u>And after Lot was separated from him, Jehovah said to Abram, Lift up your eyes now and look from the place where you</u> are northward and southward, and eastward and westward. 15 <u>For all the land which you see I will give to you, and to your seed forever.</u>

Here is Abraham being sanctified by faith, in type and shadow. He was set apart, separated from what he had brought with him so that he could see what laid before Him. He was forgetting what was behind and possessing what faith could see. Now we bring this into its new covenant counterpart. Remember the words of Christ to Paul on the road to Damascus. See if you can hear this same reality, this same story in the words of Jesus to Paul.

***Acts 26:15** ...I am Jesus whom you persecute; 16 but rise up and stand on your feet, for it is for this reason I appeared to you, to appoint you a* *servant and a witness both of what you saw, and in what I shall appear to you, 17 having delivered you from the people and the nations, to whom I now send you, 18 to open their eyes, and to turn them from darkness to light, and from the authority of Satan to God, in order that they may receive remission of sins, <u>and an inheritance among those being sanctified by faith in Me.</u>*

And remember Paul's words to the church in Ephesus as he left them for the ship.

Acts 20:32 *And now, brothers, I commend you to God and to the Word of His grace, which is able to build up and to give <u>you inheritance among all those being sanctified.</u>*

This is the very first thing that Jesus Christ says to Paul. "Paul," He says, "There is an inheritance. It is the true possessing of the heavenly land. It has to do with coming to live where I am, to see as I see, experience all that I am and have. But like your forefather Abraham, this inheritance is not possessed by sight. I'm sending you to help lift up people's eyes. I'm sending you to proclaim this inheritance for those who will be sanctified by faith in Me. Paul, whatever things that were gain to you, you will count them loss. But faith will possess a better land. Faith will possess a heavenly country and you will find yourself to be a citizen of heaven."

Do you see this reality of being sanctified by faith, sanctified in the Truth? Can you see that it is the truth that sets you apart in your heavenly country. It is the truth that strips the earth from your heart and makes you a heavenly being. The Truth of Christ revealed by the Spirit Himself. This is what caused the apostles to live in the heavens even though their vessel was bound to the earth. This is how Christ could abide in His Father even though He walked through the cities of Israel. This is how Paul was content in any natural circumstance. He was content to live on in the body, or content to have his earthen body taken from him. "For me to live is Christ, and to die is gain." Can you understand that it is the soul's apprehension of Truth that possesses the inheritance? All that is Christ is yours to inherit. And yet nothing that Christ is can be accessed and possessed and inherited without faith. You are set apart unto the universe of Christ when Truth washes away one man, and reveals Another.

I don't know that I can communicate very well how big of a deal this is. This is it. This is everything. Jesus says to His Father, "Father, everything I have is theirs. Everything I am is theirs. My glory is theirs. My love is theirs. My inheritance is theirs to share. Indeed they are co-heirs with Me. Father, I don't pray that they be taken out of the world. That is not what they need. I only pray that they be sanctified in the Truth."

So many in the church are sadly waiting to be taken out of the world in order to experience the inheritance. So many have projected into the future these present realities that are possessed by faith. Because sight cannot access them now, we assume that sight will access them later. But this is a lie. Sight will never access Christ. Faith will access Him now and forever. Faith will access and experience the glory of Jesus Christ.

Let's read again the last Scripture from the list of

those that we read earlier.

> ***2Thessalonians 2:13*** *But we ought to thank God always concerning you, brothers, beloved by the Lord, because God chose you from the beginning to salvation in sanctification of the Spirit and faith in the truth, 14 to which He called you through our gospel, to obtain the glory of our Lord Jesus Christ.*

Chapter III
The Division of the Cross

Whenever you're talking about the work of the cross, there are always two realities to keep in mind. First of all, there is what I often call the objective work of the cross. In other words, there is God's view, God's understanding of what He has accomplished once and for all time through the death, burial, and resurrection of His Son. And then, NOT in addition to that, but as a result of that, there is the personal, subjective experience of what God HAS accomplished through the cross. That subjective, personal experience works in you only and always according to the measure of Light that is shining in your soul.

In other words, God has accomplished something. He has finished something that is a fixed reality. It is unbending and unchanging. But only as that accomplishment is revealed in you, only as His great achievement – Christ crucified, buried, and raised – is revealed in you by the Spirit of Truth, do you and I have any inward experience or apprehension of it. The objective facts are established in God's eyes. The subjective experience works in us to the degree that we see with His eyes, know with His mind, and walk in His Light. In a sentence, just like the Promised Land of old, **what God has given must be possessed by faith**.

With that in mind we can understand something of sanctification. As we have said, sanctification has to do with a permanent separation. It has to do with a great division, and that division is first an accomplished, unbending reality in the mind of God. Then that division, that separation, becomes an unstoppable reality in our souls as we grow up and experience His mind. But again, first it is something that God has accomplished.

Listen to what T. Austin-Sparks says about this great divide - "God says, 'In the moment in which I turned my face from My Son on the cross, I closed forever the door to the Adam race. I abandoned the Adam race, so far as it ever had a chance of being accepted by Me or coming into My purpose'....all that God [now] has to say to the Adam race is: you must be born again."

This judgment, this great abandonment, was accomplished by the cross of Jesus Christ. When Christ said "It is finished," God drew a line and said, "I have forever divided Myself, separated Myself, from that realm, that reality, that man." That is not to say that He does not affect or intervene in the natural creation. I don't mean that He never gives direction in a decision or heals an ailing body, but He has terminated His *relationship* with that realm and that man. He has judged it, and put it out of His camp. He has raised up a boundary that forever divides between the first and the second, the old and the new, the living and the dead, the Light and the dark, Adam and Christ.

We are by nature a part of what God has abandoned. We are by nature a partaker of what God has condemned. For this reason, Christ says, "The one believing in Him is not condemned; but the one not believing <u>has already been condemned</u>" (John 3:18). John the Baptist echoes this same truth, saying, "The one believing in the Son has everlasting life; but the one disobeying the Son will not see life, but the wrath of God remains on him" (John 3:36). Paul says, "We are by nature children of wrath."

I trust we have seen these things before, but I doubt that we usually stand still and look at this boundary, this line of demarcation, long enough for the magnitude of it to hit us with full force. In other words, I don't think we can bear to look very long at just how severe a thing it is. I don't think we normally want to see the full extent of what God has left behind, because to see it would demand a response that we're not ready to make.

Above and Below

When we're talking about sanctification, we are first of all talking about the full extent of what God has divided from Himself. That's where our understanding of sanctification begins. It continues with our experience of that division. But it begins with a Spirit-given recognition of how God has divided one universe from another - the universe of Adam and the universe of Christ. There is a biblical term for each of these universes that I want to look at today - one is called "above" and the other is called "below."

As you know, your Bible uses these two words somewhat frequently. Jesus says things like, "You are from beneath; I am from above. You are of this world; I am not of this world." Or, "He who comes from above is above all; he who is of the earth is earthly and speaks of the earth. He who comes from heaven is above all." In Galatians 4, Paul says, "But the Jerusalem above is free, which is the mother of us all." In Colossians chapter 3 he says, "If then you were raised with Christ, seek those things which are above." James chapter 3 says, "This wisdom does not descend from above, but *is* earthly, sensual, demonic."

Unfortunately, our natural minds are usually quick to 'carnalize' these terms. We hear the words above and below and we immediately think of geographic, physical locations. The terms above and below aren't referring to physical locations, but rather to two opposite and contrary natures, lives, realms, orders. Rabon Byrd says, "Above is not just where He is or where He takes us, but WHO He is...If above denotes the very nature of Christ, then beneath speaks of the nature of man. What I want us to see is that above there is Christ and nothing else; Christ all and in all; but beneath it is man and nothing else."

These are terms that relate **to a *nature* and *order* of reality**. Below, that nature is adamic, and the order is the system of *natural* reality. The adamic man is governed in all things by the law of sin and death. This is the nature of the fallen adamic man. The order below is governed by created laws and systems and structures that are for the natural man. This is 'below'. Below is not a place; it is a state of being, a kind of being, a kind of reality that is summed up in the word "Adam."

Above, however, is the nature and order of God in Christ. Perhaps you are not accustomed to thinking of Christ in this way, but Jesus Christ is more than just an individual being. Of course He is the individual and only Son of God. Of course He is the Person who came as a man, was crucified, buried, and raised. But He is also the life and realm and nature into which we come to live. As such, He is a universe of truth, thought, reality, order, and love that fulfills every type and shadow and becomes the reality of every promise and blessing having to do with our inheritance. He is the land into which we come to dwell, the land which is above, the city which is above, the heavenly habitation.

In the incarnation, Jesus descended. He came down below. But that doesn't mean that He traveled any distance. That doesn't mean that He made a trip from one *place* to another. No, He descended when He took on the form of man. The journey was not from one location to another, it was from one kind to another. He descended when He became human, and He came to the world below, not just because He wanted to forgive sins. No, it's much bigger than that. Sins are dealt with through the cross, but the cross is so much bigger than a way to deal with sins.

He descended below so that He could bear in Himself the end of that man. Not a physical end, but a judicial end. Paul says that Christ became the "last Adam." He took that entire tree, that entire kind, and brought it into a judicial and eternal separation from God. It is this separation that I'm trying to get you to see. That is why He cried out, "My God, My God, why hast Thou forsaken me?" He brought the realm below into judgment, separation. In the resurrection He did not then restore the earth or the adamic man to presence of God. The resurrection is not the return of Adam, or the redemption of the first man. Christ alone was raised, and this raising from the dead is much more than we often assume. When the Scriptures talk about Christ risen from the dead, they do not only refer to Christ getting His life back, or coming back alive. In Christ's resurrection and ascension, He left the world below and returned above. He returned above having established an eternal boundary with only one blood-covered door.

In the cross of Jesus Christ, God dealt with the natural man in natural Israel under a natural covenant. He had put up with their disobedience, unbelief, and rebellion since the day He called them out of Egypt. He had put up with them for a very long time, and now, in total justice, He put them away.

> ***Romans 3:23*** *For all have sinned and fall short of the glory of God, 24 being justified freely by His grace through the redemption that is in Christ Jesus, 25 whom God set forth as a propitiation by His blood, through faith, to demonstrate His righteousness, <u>because in His forbearance God had passed over the sins that were previously committed,</u> 26 to demonstrate at the present time His righteousness, that He might be just and the justifier of the one who has faith in Jesus.*

Having tolerated the rebellion and corruption of the first man, God put that man away and separated unto Himself a new man - Christ the Firstfruits from among the dead. Christ the Head of a new corporate body. Christ the

Firstborn of a new seed, a new kind. Now, Christ was raised up out from the earth. He ascended. He sanctified Himself that we could be sanctified in Him. He left the nature and order that is called "beneath." He left the realm that He had called "below." He arose up to where He was before. He drew a line, a permanent boundary that marked out the boundaries of a new Israel, a new Jerusalem. He drew a line that marked out the boundaries of God's relationship with man. Those boundaries are the boundaries of Christ - the height the depth the width and the breadth of Christ. This is the heavenly land where we can dwell. This is the place and person and nature and order into which we are invited. Christ all and in all.

Chapter IV
Christ, the Door

When He ascended, though He forever divided the first from the second, below from above, He left a door open. He left a door with blood on it for any who wanted to ascend with Him, and the door was guarded by a cross. The door was guarded by a Cherubim with a flaming sword. You cannot pass through it and live. **And yet those who die His death are free to ascend. Those who will bear in themselves the death of Christ are called upward to a heavenly life, a heavenly place, a heavenly nature, all of which is Christ.**

> *John 1:47 Jesus saw Nathanael coming toward Him, and said of him, "Behold, an Israelite indeed, in whom is no deceit!" 48 Nathanael said to Him, "How do You know me?" Jesus answered and said to him, "Before Philip called you, when you were under the fig tree, I saw you." 49 Nathanael answered and said to Him, "Rabbi, You are the Son of God! You are the King of Israel!" 50 Jesus*

*answered and said to him, "Because I said to you, 'I saw you under the fig tree,' do you believe? You will see greater things than these." 51 And He said to him, "Most assuredly, I say to you, **hereafter you shall see heaven open**, and the angels of God ascending and descending upon the Son of Man."*

In the book of Revelation, John the Apostle writes:

***Revelation 4:1** After these things I looked, and behold**, a door standing open in heaven**. And the first voice which I heard was like a trumpet speaking with me, saying, "Come up here, and I will show you things which must take place after this." 2 Immediately I was in the Spirit; and behold, a throne set in heaven, and One sat on the throne.*

I'm trying to impress upon you the reality of what it means to be sanctified, to be set apart unto Christ. It is not simply a matter of devotion. It's not discipline or effort or zeal. It has to do with another Life to live, another place to be, another order to govern, another nature to learn. And all of these are Christ. Christ the Life, the Place, the Order, the Nature. It is the universe of Christ, high above the earth below. It is the Mountain of God's inheritance, the Land of His choosing, the City of the great king. It is Christ risen, ascended, sanctified, and set apart. **And from heaven He beckons us to arise. From heaven He calls us with the upward call of God. From heaven He declares us citizens with Himself, co-**

heirs, and He desires that we possess this Land by faith.

He would say to us today, "Lift up your eyes, church, from the place where you now are. You have been made alive, raised up, and seated with Christ in the heavens. Now lift up your eyes. Allow the Spirit of God to open the eyes of your understanding, shine the Light of Life in your soul. Look to the north, the south, the east and the west, see this great land, this unsearchable inheritance that is called Christ. Lift up your eyes, because as far as you can see I have given to you."

Remember the experience of Abraham that God used to paint for us this same picture, this exact same story. Let's read part of it again.

> ***Genesis 13:14*** *And the LORD said to Abram, after Lot had separated from him: "Lift your eyes now and look from <u>the place where you are</u>—northward, southward, eastward, and westward; 15 for all the land which you see I give to you and your seed forever...17 Arise, walk in the land through its length and its width, for I give it to you." 18 Then Abram moved his tent, and went and dwelt by the terebinth trees of Mamre, which are in Hebron, and built an altar there to the LORD.*

I'm attempting to describe something of the fixed divide between what is called below and above, but I'm also trying to set the stage for us to see something of the greatness of what the Scriptures call the "upward call of God in Christ," or sometimes it is referred to as the "high calling."

High Calling

What is your calling? Christians talk about their "calling" all the time. Unfortunately, we most often use this word to refer to personal, individual roles in the earth or in the church. And, although roles and functions in both are valid, they do not constitute a person's true calling. In other words, Paul was *called* an Apostle by the Lord, but Paul would have never considered apostleship his calling. Paul's specific function in the Lord's body had a name. That name was called Apostle, and he functioned in that role. But if you were to ask Paul about his calling, he would have said,

> ***Philippians 3:12*** *Not that I have already attained, or am already perfected; but I press on, that I may lay hold of that for which Christ Jesus has also laid hold of me. 13 Brethren, I do not count myself to have apprehended; but one thing I do, forgetting those things which are behind and reaching forward to those things which are ahead, 14 I press toward the goal for the prize of the* ***upward call of God in Christ Jesus.***

And then he adds this -

> ***Philippians 3:15*** *Therefore let us, as many as are mature, have this mind; and if in anything you think otherwise, God will reveal even this to you.*

What is the meaning of this phrase – "upward call of God in Christ Jesus?" Precisely what we've been talking about. **It is the beckoning of the Lord to our soul to abide in the heavens in Him. It is a perpetual invitation from the one who has ascended for us to ascend with Him, to be found in Him, to dwell (in our comprehension, in our awareness) where He dwells, to be with Him where He is.** Certainly we have already been translated into Him as a matter of spiritual fact, as a matter of God's view. Paul tells us that we have been translated out of the kingdom of darkness and made to dwell in the Son of His love. **But our upward call is a trumpet call to the soul, a deep summoning of the soul, to make an experiential exodus out of the earth in order to be a purely heavenly being.**

I know to the carnal mind this sounds intense, even excessive, but is it anything different than the words of Paul who said, "May it be that I would never boast except in the cross of the Lord Jesus Christ through whom the world has been crucified to me and I have been crucified to the world?" Was this merely a theological standing in Paul's mind? Was it a positional truth that awaited actual consummation? Or was this the literal experience of that man's soul. Did Paul perhaps actually experience this kind of sanctification, setting apart, separation from the nature and order that Christ called "below?"

I am obviously more than convinced that this was much more than a statement of theological position for Paul. How else could a man live as he lived and give as he gave and rejoice and rest and abide in such an otherworldly reality? There is no doubt about it. Paul was a man who was being sanctified by faith, sanctified by truth. He was a person who knew, in a deep and genuine way, how the earth can be washed from the soul with the washing of the water of the Word. He was apprehending that for which he had been apprehended. He had climbed Jacob's ladder, so to speak, into the heavens and was becoming more and more a purely heavenly man.

Don't Look Back

Sanctification is a journey of the heart, an exodus of the soul. And it involves an inward departure from one kind of land and relationship, and the discovery of another. Never forget God's first words to Abraham:

> ***Genesis 12:1** Now the LORD had said to Abram: "Get out of your country, From your family And from your father's house, To a land that I will show you.*

We just read Paul's description of the same thing. Forgetting those things which are behind, and apprehending, possessing those things which God is revealing, and walking in those things that God reveals.

And if we turn to Colossians chapter 3 we see Paul instructing the church in this same journey.

> ***Colossians 3:1** If then you were raised with Christ, seek those things which are above, where Christ is, sitting at the right hand of God. 2 Set your mind on things above, not on things on the*

earth. 3 For you died, and your life is hidden with Christ in God.

Here is this word "above" again. He begins by saying that you were raised above. It is because of what God has done, because of what the cross has accomplished in raising you above with Christ, that it is absolutely appropriate and essential for you to seek and see those things which are above, NOT the things which are on the earth. Fix your gaze there, Paul says, on the things being revealed in this heavenly land. Fix your heart on the new order and nature and land that is the universe of Christ. Do not look back to where you are from.

So many of the types and shadows that God recorded in the Old Testament tell this same story. Abraham, do not look back to your country, kindred, and father's house. Get out! And don't take anything with you. Lot, do not look back to a place that I have condemned. Escape to a better land. Israel, do not look back to your land of slavery, a land I have judged. Set your heart on the Land that I have given you. Possess that land by faith. Forget the things that are behind you, possess that which is before you.

The author of Hebrews has this to say about these Old Covenant believers:

Hebrews 11:13 *These all died in faith, not having received the promises, but having seen them afar off were assured of them, embraced them and confessed that they were strangers and pilgrims on the earth. 14 For those who say such things declare plainly that they seek a homeland. 15 And*

<u>truly if they had called to mind that country from which they had come out, they would have had opportunity to return.</u> 16 <u>But now they desire a better, that is, a heavenly country.</u> Therefore God is not ashamed to be called their God, for He has prepared a city for them.

For the Old Covenant saints, all of this was in type and shadow. We know that. But for you and I, this is literal and real. It is not NATURAL. Remember, the natural journey is the shadow. The spiritual exodus, the high calling of God in Christ, THAT is the substance. The high calling of God for us is an invitation to dwell in the heavens, to live in the sight of God, to be found in Christ. And sanctification by faith, sanctification in truth, this is our means of ascension. **We heed this calling when we allow the revelation of Christ by the Spirit of truth to awaken us to our heavenly country, and subsequently, to turn the lights out in the country of our native birth.**

Chapter V
Living in the Earth

I would like to begin talking about the believer's relationship to the earth, but if these things aren't seen to be firmly rooted in the finished work of the cross, then we would really be better off not talking about it. Whenever you get into issues of what you might call "practical aspects of Christianity," the temptation is always to turn wisdom into religion.

Translated Out of the Kingdom of Darkness

The only way for somebody like you and I to approach God is to find at the cross the end of the adamic man, and a way for our souls to participate in a totally new man, a new kind, a new seed. The cross was God's great division. It was a separation between Adam and Christ. **And even though the two may seem to blend together in our unrenewed mind, they are perfectly separated in the mind of God.**

Do you know the Scripture that talks about how our sins are put away from us as far as the east is from the west? God accomplished that by putting Adam away from Himself as far as the east is from the west. So you and I are not redeemed and reconciled Adams. You and I are partakers of the divine nature, born of God's Spirit, translated out of one side of that separation and made to dwell in the other. "You have been translated out of the kingdom of darkness and made to dwell in the Son of His love."

That is the fact of sanctification. That is something of what Jesus meant when He said, "Father, for this reason I sanctify Myself." "What are you separating yourself from, Jesus?" the disciples might have asked. "I'm separating Myself from you and your world, and going back to My Father." Philip says, "Wait! Don't do that! Stay with us!" And Jesus says, "No, it's actually better that I go back to the Father, because I am making a way for you to be where I am. I am making a way for you to be with Me in the Father. You will be no longer of this world even as I am no longer of this world." But Philip panics and says, "But we don't even know the way out! Or the way in!" Jesus reassures him, "Philip, I am the Way, the Truth, and the Life, nobody comes to the Father but by Me."

Can you see what was going on there that night before Christ's crucifixion? Jesus was not just getting ready to fly off to heaven. No, He was bringing the entire world below, the entire man beneath, into His death, and permanently separating it from the Father. **And yet, in doing so, He was providing Himself as an eternal door out, and an eternal way in. He was providing Himself as a habitation for any who would desire to live in and by His life.**

You see, this is why it is such lunacy for Christians to

think that they have a life to live for God. That is why it is so silly for us to assume that God wants us to modify our lives and make them fit for His presence. We don't live in His presence. Christ does, and we are hidden with Christ in God. You have died and your life is hidden with Christ in God. "I am in the Father, you are in Me, and I am in you." Hide here in the cleft of My Rock and I will cover you with My hand. And there, when all that you are by nature is out of My site, there you can experience My glory.

Adam is never reconciled to God. Adam cannot live in God's sight. Adam is left on the other side of the eternal chasm, and so for you and I to know what is real, we must learn Christ. To know what God has done, we must learn Christ. To know who and where and why we exist, and what it means to serve God, we must learn Christ. We must learn to know and live the life that God has restored to Himself. We must abide in the life He has accepted. We must offer Him the fruit of the Seed He has planted for a harvest.

The Love of God

The greatest thing that God ever did for you is to judge you and separate you from Himself in the cross of Jesus Christ. Only in the complete and utter pitch blackness of the carnal mind could someone not recognize *this* to be the great love and grace of God. The kindest thing that God could have done for you is to give you a death and judgment in His Son that had a door attached to it. **He gave you a separation that became the end of His relationship to you in the flesh, so that it**

could also be the beginning of His relationship to you in the Spirit. A division that was the end of His relationship to you by the Law, so that He could have relationship with you as a partaker of His life. An end of His relationship to you in the earth, so that He could now relate to you in the heavens.

People today are crying out for God to have some sort of relationship with them in the flesh. We want Him to touch our natural bodies. We want Him to fix our stuff when it's broken. We want Him to prove that He likes us just the way we are. But if we had any light at all, if there was even a flicker of light in our hearts to see, we would fall on our face and thank God Almighty that He has ended His relationship to us in the flesh and offered us a relationship with Him in His Son.

This separation is good news. This separation is the love of God. Because in judging the world, He simultaneously offers them salvation. In putting them away, He also creates a way to bring them into Himself. Hosea the prophet spoke of it hundreds of years before God accomplished it.

> ***Hosea 5:14*** *[the LORD says] For I will be like a lion to Ephraim, And like a young lion to the house of Judah. I, even I, will tear them and go away; I will take them away, and no one shall rescue.* ***Hosea 6:1*** *Come, and let us return to the LORD; For He has torn, but He will heal us; He has stricken, but He will bind us up. 2 After two days He will revive us;* <u>*On the third day He will raise us up, That we may live in His sight.*</u>

He tears us and goes away. He takes Adam away with no one to rescue. And yet, there is a door left open. We can say, "Come let us return to the Lord. He's torn us, but He will heal us. He has put us away, and yet on the third day we can rise up and live in His sight." What a prophecy! What a view of our salvation!

We can see the same picture in the captivity of Israel in Babylon. God casts them out of His sight. God tells them to bow their neck to Nebuchadnezzar, the king of Babylon. He tells them to go into judgment out of His presence, out of His land, and face their end. And yet, those who will turn to Him, those who will turn in faith to see Him, they will return. They will find the blood covered door left open. They will find what Isaiah calls the Highway of Holiness, and they will return to the Lord. They will cross over the great divide and come home to Zion.

Isaiah 35:8 *A highway shall be there, and a road, And it shall be called the Highway of Holiness. The unclean shall not pass over it, But it shall be for others. Whoever walks the road, although a fool, Shall not go astray. 9 No lion shall be there, Nor shall any ravenous beast go up on it; It shall not be found there. But the redeemed shall walk there, 10 And the ransomed of the LORD shall return, And come to Zion with singing, With everlasting joy on their heads. They shall obtain joy and gladness, And sorrow and sighing shall flee away.*

God judges a people in wrath by the hands of Nebuchadnezzar. He utterly wipes them out and separates them from His land. And yet a way is made for the great restoration and reconciliation and redemption of Israel. It's a resurrection to Zion, something they have never known. **Not their restoration to a national and natural relationship, but Christ's restoration to His Father, and their participation in that homecoming.**

This is the foundation. Everything else hinges on understanding this separation, and our calling to be separated. First we must understand the division that God established, and only then can we understand what it means to be sanctified. Being separated unto the Lord is first of all a matter of crossing the great divide in the Person of Christ, and living hidden with Him in the Father.

Chapter VI
The Journey

The question arises, if we have passed over that great divide with and in the person of Christ, what then is our journey? What is it that must now happen with us? The Bible describes this in many ways. In one place it is called coming to know even as we are known. In another it is coming to apprehend that for which we have been apprehended of God. In yet another it is the inward putting off of what God has put away, and the inward putting on of what God has established. The language of Paul that is particularly pressed upon my heart is "the upward call of God in Christ," or the "high calling."

The journey of the Christian soul is never to ascend somewhere that we have not yet come. On the contrary, **the journey of the believer's soul is always to see and apprehend and learn to live in the realm and life and land that is Christ**. So many people today far underestimate what God has already finished, and therefore they far overstate what it is that man is capable of doing. God has finished this division. God has drawn

His boundary. Christ has sanctified Himself. He rose from among the dead and ascended, and He left a man and a creation behind. That was finished once and forever.

So as far as the work is concerned, the journey of the soul is over as soon as it begins. You and I were *immediately* translated out of one man and into another. We were immediately taken from one kind and creation and translated into Christ Himself. You HAVE died and your life IS hidden with Christ in God. What does that leave for us? What is the growth of a soul? Just one thing. **We see the Place where we are, and leave another place behind. We learn the Life that we have, and let the other fall back to the other side of God's great divide. We behold the land of Christ by faith and never look back to Egypt, to Sodom, to our country, kindred, and father's house.** In other words, we become mindful of those things above, and not those things which are on the earth.

This is the upward call of God in Christ. It is a calling into Christ, into the Life of Christ and into the knowing of Christ. That call to move in becomes our moving out. This is why he calls it the high calling, or the upward call. He understood this calling to be, in the truest sense of these words, an exodus from the world below to dwell in Christ above. All of this was taking place in Paul long before his physical body died. To a great degree, Paul was a heavenly man long before his body returned to the dust.

A Greater View

Like everything else when you are learning Christ, you think you've seen something clearly, and then the Lord eventually brings you back again for another look. This time around you see an even greater view. It doesn't contradict what you saw the last time the Lord was dealing with your heart on a particular issue. In fact, it should confirm it. But it also swallows it up into an even greater view. Something else of Christ, some other aspect of Him, comes into your field of vision. And your heart is further adjusted to the truth. It's a bit like a chiropractor putting your spine back where it needs to be. That's the way truth works on your heart. You see a greater view of Him and things pop and snap and shift into a true alignment - an alignment with the truth.

The last time that the Lord had my heart looking at this division, this separation, it seemed to me that the primary focus was what I was coming IN to. I mean, I didn't see much at that time about what it meant to come OUT. The focus had everything to do with coming in. And for certain, without a question in my heart, the coming in is the far greater deal. Coming into Christ is the greatness of our salvation. You have heard me say before that the greatness of our salvation is not measured by what we come out of, but rather what or WHO we come into.

That is certainly true, and I'm not questioning that at all. But still, there is the fact that things are left behind. Still, in coming into the land, and seeing the greatness of the Land and the inheritance through Isaac and all the promises, still there was the fact that Abraham LEFT a country and kindred and father's house. It's the same with Israel crossing the Red Sea, and crossing the Jordan. Without question, the greatness of their salvation was the priesthood and kingdom that they were brought into. The greatness of their salvation was not the dead Egyptians or the defeated Pharaoh. It was being brought into a relationship that God recognized as "Israel my Son, even my Firstborn." <u>And yet</u>, there was also the fact that Egypt was left behind. There was the constant thorn in Israel's side that had to do with the people not truly *leaving* Egypt in their hearts.

This time, with me, the emphasis of the Lord seems to be on what it means to leave Egypt behind. This time the spotlight seems to be not just on what it means to be a heavenly man, but also on what it means to ascend with Christ and leave the world below. Paul said of himself that he was crucified to the world and the world was crucified to him. What did that mean to him? How did that work in him?

Now before I say anything else, let me remind you of the warning I gave in the introduction. What I want to say can be easily misunderstood. If we're going to talk about abiding in the heavens and cutting ties with the earth, then it is essential that we are first rooted and grounded in a Spirit-given view of what that entails, and what it doesn't entail. In other words, we have to have seen the judgment, the division that was established by the cross.

The reason I say that is because for about 8 years of my life I did everything I could think of to cut my ties with the earth. I recognized that I was bound to the earth in so many ways. I recognized that my heart was full of pride and greed and lust and all sorts of needs and addictions to things in the earth. And therefore, in an attempt to be more spiritual, you could say in an attempt to be more of a heavenly man, I started to try to cut myself loose from the earth. I threw away my T.V. and I never watched movies. I didn't think those things were inherently bad, but I didn't want my heart strings attached to the earth. I chose not to read certain things, or go certain places, or drink various beverages. On top of that, I didn't date. I joined the "Bachelor Until the Rapture" club. I fasted food on a regular basis. I fasted sleep. I even tried to fast talking. I won't continue with this story because it only gets more embarrassing.

Here's my point - I had no idea what it actually meant to abide in Christ, to live in the heavens. And therefore, no matter what I did to free myself from the earth, regardless how radical it sounded or how disciplined I was, it never accomplished a single thing. **I only ever replaced one natural thing for another. I let go of one natural thing and grabbed hold of something else natural, but something that I called spiritual. In other words, I stopped doing something in the earth in order that I could start doing something in religion.** I never made any "progress" because I had yet to see what progress was. I had yet to see God's great divide. I didn't know what the cross accomplished, where Christ was, what it meant that I was in Him, or what it meant for me to heed the upward call of God in Christ Jesus.

Let me try to say this another way. **It is a foolish and futile thing to try to let go of your relationship with the earth when you haven't even started to see the heavens. It's a pointless thing to try to sever your ties with the adamic nature when you haven't begun to see the life of Christ by faith. What you'll end up doing is swapping one natural carnal thing for another. You'll let go of something you call worldly and grab hold of**

something you call heavenly, but they will both be worldly. They will both be carnal, and one will be religious.

That is why what I am about to say could be easily misunderstood. The Spirit of truth has to define the two realms, and the Spirit has to draw the line between what is of Adam and what is of Christ. Then you can begin to understand the inward journey of leaving the one and possessing the other by faith. Without that foundation, you just wander in the vast wilderness of man's religious ideas.

It is foolish to try to break ties with the earth when you haven't seen the heavens. But here's the other side of that - **it is also foolish, it is also vanity, for us to hold onto the earth when we've begun to see the heavens.** I said a lot of things to get to that statement, but it's not the kind of statement that you can just say without carefully placing it where it belongs and where it makes sense. Sooner or later in growing up in the Lord, it seems that the Lord begins to deal with the heart about letting go of the earth.

Honestly, I don't really like to get into specifics with this kind of thing. In my opinion, it has to be something that the Lord makes clear in each individual heart. I only want to say a few very general things. **Truth eventually comes into view in such a way, and to such an extent, that a person begins to recognize where and how the world is pulling us downward.** I'm not talking about bad behaviors and obvious immorality issues. That stuff should be obvious. I'm talking about things that are permissible but not beneficial, things that are absolutely legitimate in the earth, but that begin to feel like an anchor keeping your heart and mind and attention on the wrong life and in the wrong realm.

As we heed the upward call of God in Christ, sooner or later we begin to recognize something of the extent to which we have invested in the earth. We have sown to the earth and reaped a harvest of responsibilities, connections, and emotional and relational ties. This is obviously normal for a natural man, but it starts to feel a bit abnormal for one who is going on with the Lord. Light begins to expose these things and call them to your attention, and perfectly normal and legitimate natural things are seen in a different way. They are seen with a different value system. The question is not whether this or that is evil. The question is not whether something makes you feel guilty or ashamed or compromising. It's not really that at all. The question is simply which side of God's great divide are these things on. Which side of the line are they a part of, and to which side are they pulling my heart, my gaze, my attention.

What would it be like if all of our investments, the things that really have our heart, our attention, our focus - what if all of our investments were in Christ? What if, rather than reaping from the earth a harvest of responsibilities and concerns and preoccupations and needs, we reaped from Christ a harvest of Truth and reality that made the earth seem comparatively small and trivial?

Do you feel the Lord dealing with your heart to begin to invest less in the world of shadows? Again, I'm not talking about any of the reasons and motivations that may have brought these things to your attention in the past. I'm not talking about guilt or reward. I'm simply talking about the Truth. I'm talking about the great divide that exists between "below" and "above," and how Christ has set Himself apart, sanctified Himself, in order that we might also be sanctified in Him. I submit these things to you for your consideration.

T. Austin-Sparks says,

> *Relationships are entirely changed on resurrection ground. Mary would gladly have touched Him in the garden, would have embraced Him, but He said: "Touch me not..." In effect: "Things are changed; the holding of before is no longer. A different realm has been entered, a different relationship. Yes! still your Lord, still your Savior, still your Friend, but a difference. I am not to be held as though I belonged to this earth; I am not to be taken hold of, as though this were My place." "Touch me not; for I am not yet ascended unto the Father." The first thing in resurrection is the recognition of our heavenly relationship, not our earthly relationship. All that is heavenly now makes first claim and what is earthly, even in a religious way, has to be put back. (There is a good deal of earthly religiousness, and religious earthliness. There is a good deal in religion, that is earthly and of this world: earth bound and of man). Resurrection union cuts clean and clear of everything that belongs to this world, even though it may be religious. What is only of God has a testimony in this world; it has no other relationship. Its business here is merely to testify in the world, but to have no other kind of tie.*

Resurrection represents the completeness of our separation from the world. "If then you be raised together with Christ, seek the things that are above..." In other words, to all that is here: "Touch me not; My Father has first claim." That is a most elementary thing, but it is true. It means that heaven has first and primary claim upon everything, because now all relationships are heavenly, all interests are heavenly. That is a position essential to God's end. We know quite well, in the practical outworking of this truth, that in the degree in which any believer has a voluntary relationship to this world, or is held by anything of this world, that believer is stunted in his spiritual development. The world is an obstruction to the fullness of Christ. It becomes impossible to go on if there is a bit of the world holding. Putting that round the other way; it is just wonderful, amazing, and blessedly joyous to notice how those who really do go on with the Lord spontaneously drop the world.

Chapter VII
The Great Divide

Sanctification is a reality that begins with what God has separated from Himself. I think there are a lot of Christians who never consider the fact that God has permanently judged, and separated the adamic man and world from Himself. We assume that the cross simply forgave that world and its shortcomings. Or we are still waiting for God to fix the natural world and all of the evil in it. So many of our prayers and hopes and ministries are directed towards this end. We want God to fix Adam and the adamic world.

But the cross of Jesus Christ has nothing to do with fixing the adamic man or the adamic world. The cross of Jesus Christ only fixed *God's relationship* to that world, and it accomplished that by judging it in His death and eternally separating it from relatedness with God. Adam and his earth continue in the natural realm, but Adam and his earth will never again have relationship with God. God has forever fixed a boundary between Himself and that man. The only way that you and I can ever have relationship with God is to be born of His Spirit, made alive with Him, raised up with Christ, translated with Christ from one world to another - out from the universe of Adam and into the universe of Christ. **The only way to ever cross God's eternal boundary is through the blood covered door where we die with Christ and receive His resurrection as our own life.**

Sanctification starts there. It starts with this great divide. It starts with God dividing the adamic world and man from Himself, and, as we have seen, sanctification then becomes the experience of the Christian believer wherein we are separated from all that God has put away from Himself. And we are separated unto all that God has brought to Himself. These things are not really two separate things, or two separate definitions. There is the great separation that God has brought about through the cross, and then there is our inward experience of that very same separation as we begin to walk in the Light.

I'm trying to make sure that we understand the nature and reality of this division. God will still touch the earth, but He does not have relationship with it. He has no covenant with it. He put away the covenant that involved the natural man in natural Israel. Hebrews tells us that He put away the first in order to establish the second. He made the first obsolete when He established a New Covenant, an everlasting covenant, with the Israel that is His Son and the people who live in that Son. **God will still touch the earth, but only to turn your hearts to the heavens. God will involve Himself in the earth at times, in what we call miracles or revivals or signs, but He does these things only in ways that invite us to leave the earth, be crucified to the earth, and dwell in His Son.**

We think the purpose of God is in the miracle, but the miracle was given for a much greater purpose. The purpose of the miracle was to point beyond the great divide where we must learn to live. We think the revival was the purpose, and we're always confused when they come and go. But the revival was not the purpose; it was given *with purpose*. That purpose was to invite the soul out from the realm in which the revival occurred. God has no true relationship or covenant with the adamic world. When He touches that world He does so with purpose, and that purpose is not for the natural world. The purpose is always to heed the upward call of God in Christ to cross the divide and dwell above. Since you have risen with Christ, fix your eyes on things above, not on things that are on the earth.

As we begin to understand the nature of God's relationship to the earth, we then have our hearts in the right place for the Spirit of God to deal with us about *our* relationship to the earth. That world fell from purpose, fell from glory, and fell into sin and death. Christ took that world of fallen humanity upon Himself and separated it from the Father. As I said previously, like the scapegoat in the Old Testament, Christ took upon Himself that entire kind and brought it permanently outside the camp. That is called judgment.

Then Christ separated Himself from it. He had no more business with that man, that realm, that covenant. He had fulfilled it all, brought it to a realization in Himself, and so He left. He arose and ascended. But He did not arise or ascend alone - He brought many sons to glory. He led captivity captive, ascended to the Father with a people that were born of His Spirit. The head came out from the womb of death first, but it was attached to a body that shared its life. Zion travailed and gave birth, and a nation was born in a day. Paul says, we were made alive together, raised together, and seated together with Christ in the heavenlies.

So, regardless of what any of us sees or comprehends, regardless of what we have even heard proclaimed to us, we have crossed the eternal divide in the person of Jesus Christ. We have come to the Father's House where He has prepared a place for us in Himself. He prepared that place through His death, burial, and resurrection. That is how He made room for us in Himself, in the Father. You have died and your life is hidden with Christ in God. Again, even if a Christian has seen nothing of this by faith, it is still true. Even if a Christian has heard nothing of this preached to their ears, it doesn't change what they are, where they are, how God knows them, and how God has ceased to know them. Just as Paul says in Romans, they are dead to the world, dead to Adam, and alive to God in Christ.

This journey of sanctification, as we have been talking about, is not about arriving anywhere, but rather living in the reality and realm where we *have* arrived. The process of sanctification that works in you and I is not a process whereby we gain something that we had yet to receive. It is rather where we learn to walk and live and know the life and place and reality that is Christ. In a very real sense we can be said to be sanctified immediately upon new birth. That is where we have passed out of one man and into another. But also in a very real sense, it can be said (and it is said in Scripture) that we are BEING sanctified by the truth, sanctified by faith, BEING set apart in our souls to live where our life is. To walk where our home is, and to see where salvation has brought us.

Abraham's Journey

As far as our experience of sanctification is concerned, we are talking exclusively about learning to live where we really are. It means walking the breadth and length and width of the land that is Christ, and leaving another behind. My heart is stuck on God's first words to Abraham. It keeps playing over and over again in my heart. "<u>Get out!</u> Get out of your country, kindred, and father's house, and go unto a land that I will show you."

When I was thinking about this verse, the question came to me, why did God say it like that? Why didn't he just tell Abraham to leave? Why did he mention the country, kindred, and father's house? What is there for us to see? And as I was pondering that I started to see in a new way that God's call to leave was comprehensive. It involved leaving behind all that Abraham would have called his own. His country – the land where he was born and the place that was familiar to him. His kindred – the relationships that he knew and the people that he understood to be family. And His father's house – which I understand to mean his inheritance. All that was his to inherit, all that was his to possess from his natural father and birthright. Abraham, leave the place, the relationships, and the inheritance that you call yours. Go unto another place, another kind of relationship, and another inheritance that all must be shown to you.

That was the beginning of Abraham's journey. That

wasn't somewhere in the middle of it. That wasn't something God said to him at the pinnacle of his maturity. This was how the journey *started*. God was straightforward from the start. These were His very first words to this man as far as we know. "Abraham, understand something from the very outset. You are leaving behind what you know and receiving something that I know. In fact, Abraham, knowing what I know will involve forgetting what you know. Knowing what I am putting before you will involve forgetting what lies behind. Abraham, everything you bring with you will be dealt with at My altar. Everything you try to take will eventually be separated from you as it is already separated from Me." This is all extremely important to consider.

We can see here how a soul is separated unto God, how we are sanctified. We are sanctified in the truth of what God has done. Sanctified by the faith that sees God's finished work. Sanctified and separated from one man and his realm, and separated unto another Man and all that He sees.

Remember, **when we're talking about ways that our relationship to the earth changes in practical ways, it must always be the result and consequence of what we are seeing in the heavens. In other words, the dying of the adamic man in our hearts must always be the byproduct of seeing and learning the heavenly Man, Christ.** If we attempt to cut ties with the earth when we are not truly seeing the heavens then we will only replace one earthly thing for another. If we try to put off the adamic man and his nature from our hearts before we begin to see Christ and understand the nature of our upward call in Him, then we will stop one thing that we call carnal only to replace it with something else that is religious and equally carnal. Man cannot escape the power and hold of the flesh through determination and discipline. That's like trying to lift yourself off the ground. Have you ever tried to wrap your arms around yourself and lift yourself off the ground? It doesn't work. Even if you were as strong as an elephant, it wouldn't work. And that is precisely what it is like when Adam tries to fix Adam, or when Adam tries to die to the flesh. Adam will not change simply because we start to hate Adam. Adam is put off when we start to see Christ as our life.

It is only when we are learning Christ by the Spirit, when we are seeing Him and growing in the true knowledge of Him, it is THEN that the Lord begins to make certain aspects of the earth start to feel contrary to what we are and what He is doing in us. It is when we are learning Christ that we can really begin to recognize and turn from those things which are not Christ.

Walking in the Spirit

As the truth becomes more and more real in the heart, sooner or later a soul that is going on with the Lord begins to recognize various ways that they are allowing the world to pull them downward. I'm not talking about outwardly immoral behavior or obviously sinful activities or attitudes. I am talking about things that are permissible but not beneficial. I'm talking about things that are legitimate in the earth, but not a part of the heavens. I'm talking about sanctification. And eventually the main question in the heart with regard to our relationship with the earth is not, "Are these things sinful?" but rather, "What side of the great divide are these things on? Where does all of this keep my heart and my attention? Has this become an anchor in my heart that holds me down from the upward call of God in Christ?"

With all of this in mind, let's look at a passage in Galatians. Everything we have been talking about is right here in Galatians chapter 5. Here we see the finished work of the cross, the two realms and realities divided from one another, and the call to walk in the one and be loosed from the other.

> ***Galatians 5:16*** *I say then: Walk in the Spirit, and you shall not fulfill the lust of the flesh. 17 For the flesh lusts against the Spirit, and the Spirit against the flesh; and these are contrary to one another, so that you do not do the things that you wish. 18 But if you are led by the Spirit, you are not under the law. 19 Now the works of the flesh are evident, which are: adultery, fornication, uncleanness...etc. 22 But the fruit of the Spirit is love, joy, peace, longsuffering, kindness, goodness, faithfulness, 23 gentleness, self-control. Against such there is no law. 24 And those who are Christ's have crucified the flesh with its passions and desires. 25 If we live in the Spirit, let us also walk in the Spirit.*

When Paul talks about flesh and Spirit here, he's not talking about two different kinds of behavior. These aren't two different ways to act. He's talking about two totally different kinds of life. Two different men, two contrary natures. Walking in the one means leaving the other behind. The two are contrary to each other and they pull against each other. The flesh lusts against the spirit and the spirit against the flesh.

Sometimes people read passages like this and don't see the enormous divide between these two things, flesh and spirit. In other words, Christians sometimes think that walking in the Spirit has to do with simply following where the Spirit is pointing, or taking instructions from God, but no, it's not like that. Walking in the Spirit isn't taking our instructions from the Lord. It's finding our Life, our reality, our country and kindred and father's house in the Lord, as the Lord. It's seeing as He sees, walking where He is, living in the Light of what He has done.

Think about this for a minute - what is walking in the flesh? Is it just a matter of checking in with the flesh during a 15 minute morning quiet time? For us to walk in the flesh, does that require some daily discipline where we try to get a feel for what the flesh wants today? No, that's silly. We all know it's a much bigger and deeper reality than that. Walking in the flesh has to do with living in and by a *nature* that defines what is real to you. How do we walk in the flesh? It's perfectly natural and effortless when we are seeing with fleshly eyes, desiring fleshly things, understanding with a carnal mind, and relating to our environment with five natural senses. Walking in the flesh has to do with where you think you are, what you think you are, and what you think is good, true, real, and right. It's a deep and comprehensive worldview. It is a nature and reality that permeates every pore of your being.

Therefore, what is walking in the Spirit? Walking in

the Spirit is exactly the same thing with the exact opposite nature and order. Walking in the Spirit has to do with living in and by ANOTHER nature that defines what is real to you. Walking in the Spirit involves seeing with the Spirit's eyes, discerning eternal and spiritual reality, and understanding with the mind of the Lord. Faith accesses the grace in which we stand. When we walk by faith, or walk in the Spirit, we are simply talking about living where we know ourself to be, living according to what we know we are, and what we think is good and true and real and right. It, too, is a nature that permeates every pore of our being and defines the nature and order of our existence.

Neither one of these take effort. Neither walking in the flesh or walking in the Spirit are a matter of effort. They are both a matter of awareness, light, consciousness. **You will live the life that you are seeing. You will walk in the realm that is real to you. And consequently, you will be free from what you are not seeing, and what has ceased to be real to you. That is the heart of sanctification.**

This is why Paul says in Galatians, "Walk in the Spirit and you shall not fulfill the lust of the flesh." He doesn't say, "Walk in the Spirit, and for heaven's sake, try harder not to fulfill the lust of the flesh." Can you see the difference? **The awareness of the one becomes the end of the other. The consciousness and experience of the one becomes the separation from the other. When the Spirit becomes what you see and what is real to you, the desires of the flesh are crowded out. They lose their power and relevance and pull because you feel very unrelated to that realm and that man.** Like Christ, who left that world and divided Himself from it, you too start to feel sanctified, set apart, by a living faith.

That is why he says in verse 18 that the one led by the Spirit is not under the law. The one who is walking in the Spirit does not need a law to tell him how to behave in the flesh. The one who walks in the Spirit is crucified to the flesh, dead to it, unrelated to the man who needed law and yet always disobeyed the law. If we walk in the Spirit we are free from the law because the nature and order of Christ becomes the Life that operates in us. This is what Paul means in Romans when he says,

> **Romans 7:4** *Therefore, my brethren, you also have become dead to the law through the body of Christ, that you may be married to another—to Him who was raised from the dead, that we should bear fruit to God. 5 For when we were in the flesh, the sinful passions which were aroused by the law were at work in our members to bear fruit to death. 6 But now we have been delivered from the law, having died to what we were held by, so that we should serve in the newness of the Spirit and not in the oldness of the letter.*

> **Romans 8:3** *For what the law could not do in that it was weak through the flesh, God did by sending His own Son in the likeness of sinful flesh, on account of sin: He condemned sin in the flesh, 4 that the righteous requirement of the law might be fulfilled in us who do not walk according to the flesh but according to the Spirit.*

Walking in the Spirit isn't something that we strive to do any more than bearing fruit is something that we strive to do. Both of these, Paul says, are the byproduct of sanctification – knowing and experiencing the divide of the cross. These things are the natural result of seeing where we are and forgetting where we were, or becoming aware of one Life and not looking back upon the other.

Again, there is the *fact* of what God has accomplished. In Galatians 5 Paul says it like this, "Those who are Christ's <u>have</u> crucified the flesh with its passions and desires." That's the fact of the great divide. That is what we now are, where God sees us. But what else does Paul say? He speaks to us of the personal journey of learning to live where we are. "If we live by the Spirit, let us also walk in the Spirit." It's all right here in these verses.

Chapter VIII
Seek Those Things Which are Above

***Colossians 3:1** If then you were raised with Christ, seek those things which are above, where Christ is, sitting at the right hand of God. 2 Set your mind on things above, not on things on the earth. 3 For you died, and your life is hidden with Christ in God. 4 When Christ who is our life appears, then you also will appear with Him in glory. 5 Therefore put to death your members which are on the earth: fornication, uncleanness, passion, evil desire, and covetousness, which is idolatry.*

This last sentence is very interesting. Paul says, "Therefore, put to death your members which are on the earth." That is exactly what this process of sanctification results in. It results in you becoming dead to the realm that Christ has died to. You become dead and you feel dead to the things that are on the other side of the divide.

"Therefore," Paul says. In other words, in light of what you are seeing while fixing your mind above, in light of what is happening when Christ your life is revealed, put to death the part of you that still resides in the earth. Allow the truth to change the nature of the relationship that you have with the realm that God has divided from Himself. Let your seeing of the heavens change your experience of the earth.

Only your fleshly body remains in the earth. Here Paul calls it our "members." Our tent. Our earthen vessel. He's not talking about the body dying. He's not talking about putting that vessel to death. He's talking about you becoming more and more dead to the realm of the vessel. **Only our body remains in the earth. Therefore, do not let the realm of the body also be the realm and life that is most real to your soul. Do not live as a body that has a soul. Live as a heavenly soul that still has a body.** Let the truth put to death the members of your body in such a way that you are not moved or motivated or consumed with and invested in the life and realm of the flesh. Let the truth set you free from it. See Christ, and allow your soul to be sanctified in His Word, set apart unto His world, and dead to all else.

When we're talking about sanctification, like any and every spiritual term, we're talking about a particular view of Christ. I don't know if you've thought about it like this or not, but every spiritual term in your Bible represents a particular view of Christ. Paul writes in 1 Corinthians chapter 1:30, "Christ is made unto you wisdom and righteousness and sanctification and redemption." These are NOT different Christian topics to discuss. These are individual views of the one Christ. Christ is all of these things, and we come to know each of these things as we see and experience Christ in these particular roles and ways. When we don't see Christ, we chop these terms up into separate theological pieces, as though they each are unique entities in themselves. We separate them from each other and teach them as individual doctrines and concepts and themes - things like sanctification, or glory, or heaven, or truth, or love, or righteousness.

I remember a time when I used to study each of these topics as individual concepts. I read books or listened to teachings on all of these things and would have told you that they were all a part of Christianity. But I didn't know them at all as aspects or facets of Christ Himself. These things are not things; they are a particular view and experience of Jesus Christ, and each of them brings something unique of Christ into view.

For example, wisdom is not what Christ teaches; it is something that Christ is, and wisdom is known by us when Christ shows us Himself. That word is perhaps more obvious. What about the word *heaven*? Heaven is not just where Christ lives. Heaven cannot be separated from Christ Himself. Heaven has to do with a particular view of Christ in His separateness from the earth, the natural, and the temporal. Heaven, not the sky or the atmosphere, but the heaven into which we have been raised with Christ, in Christ, is a particular view by faith. We come to know ourselves raised up with Him, seated with Him, and joined to Him in the heavens.

Well, sanctification is the same kind of thing. Sanctification is not some THING that God is trying to do with us, or some activity that we need to concede to. Sanctification is not an effort we put forth, or a doctrine we need to study and apply. Sanctification is our experience of Christ. It is our experience of being found in Him, being separated unto Him and separated in our hearts away from all that He is not, and away from all that He no longer sees. Sanctification is our heart's participation in Christ by faith.

Yes, it has to do with spiritual growth. Yes, it ultimately has to do with our relationships to the earth. But Christians are always trying to figure out how to grow and change our relationship to the earth long before we even see what sanctification is. We try to *do* sanctification, or *obey the rules* of sanctification, rather than seeing Him who is made unto us sanctification. This is very important to understand.

Don't ever try to be sanctified. Simply seek to know Christ by the revelation of His Spirit and you will see Him as the substance of that word. Don't ever try to glorify God. Know Christ, and when Christ is revealed you will be revealed together with Him in glory. Behold the Lord, and you will be transformed into the same image from glory to glory. Don't ever try to learn spiritual wisdom. Know Christ, and you will see and abide in the wisdom of God.

Being Found in Him

If I were to summarize in one sentence what we've talked about so far, I might say that we have seen that **sanctification is the experience of being found in Him, and ceasing to be found anywhere else**. Abraham, get out of your country, kindred, and father's house and go unto a Land that I will show you. That is the verse from Genesis chapter 12 that we read earlier. That is a natural version of what sanctification feels like. It feels like leaving one life and realm and reality behind, and it feels like awakening in another that is altogether different. It feels like leaving one country – the familiar first creation. It feels like leaving our kindred – not literally moving away from family members, but finding a far more real set of brothers, sisters, and Father. It feels like turning away from the inheritance of the earth, the inheritance of our natural father's house, and discovering another that must be shown to us.

Sanctification is our participation in Christ where the truth shows us what is now, shows us where we now are, what is now real, and crucifies our hearts to all that the cross has left behind. We've seen that this is both a finished work of God through the cross, and it is a present and ongoing experience of our soul because we are learning Christ as our life, and slowly letting go of the lie.

It is not a journey for us because God is still working on His eternal plan. No. Christ finished that plan. It is finished in Him. Ephesians 3:11 says, "The eternal purpose of God has been accomplished in Christ Jesus the Lord." But here is the question that I have been trying to present for your consideration. Here is the question I am hoping the Lord has been stirring in your heart - **Are we like Paul who had only one cry in His heart – to be found in Christ? To forget what God had forgotten? And to lay hold, by faith, of what God had given?**

Chapter IX
Crossing the Jordan

Why weren't the Israelites able to enter into the Land after coming out of Egypt? We probably all think we know the answer to that question, but let's look at it again for a minute. What was the issue? They grumbled. But that wasn't the problem. That was a symptom. They disobeyed, rebelled, complained, and wanted to go back. But all of those were symptoms of the problem. What was the root? What was the heart of their problem?

The author of Hebrews tells us plainly in chapters 3 and 4.

> ***Hebrews 3:12*** *Watch, brothers, lest perhaps there shall be in any one of you an evil heart of unbelief in withdrawing from the living God. ...19 And we see that they were not able to enter in because of **unbelief**. 4:1 Therefore, since a promise remains of entering His rest, let us fear lest any of you seem to have come short of it. 4:2 For indeed the gospel was preached to us as well as to them; but the word which they heard did not*

*profit them, **not being mixed with faith** in those who heard it.*

Here is the issue: **the land, the inheritance, was guarded by faith. It was protected by faith.** The crossing of the Red Sea had given them the right to that land, but the Jordan River stood there like a barrier that *only faith could cross.* The Jordan River is not a large river. It is easily cross-able in the natural, but it stood as an impenetrable barricade from the Lord's perspective. The walls of Jericho had fallen flat before Israel. **But the people could not even cross a small river when the land behind that river was guarded by faith.**

Do you see what I mean by "guarded by faith?" Sight would have accomplished nothing on the other side of the Jordan. Sight would have gotten them killed by the Canaanites. Sight would have possessed nothing of this land. But faith, the mind of the Lord, spiritual sight, *this* is how everything was possessed. **Only when we come to see with the mind of the Lord can we access what only He can see.**

The Israelites could see the other side of the Jordan River with their eyes. They had heard God describe the other side with their ears, but they could not cross this impenetrable boundary unless they entered in by faith into God's view. The word that they heard did not profit them because it was not mixed with faith. By faith, I do not mean strong belief or deep convictions. Faith is a Spirit-given view in God's light. It is the miracle of God sharing His perspective, His mind, His understanding with the hearts of those who will die to their own perspective, mind, and understanding.

You Have Not Gone This Way Before

In order to demonstrate what it takes to cross into the Land, God had the Israelites cross the Jordan in a very specific way. He didn't just have Joshua lift up his staff and part the river. No, that's how they exit Egypt, but that's not how they enter the land. He didn't build a bridge. He didn't let them all wade across. That certainly would have been quicker, but that wouldn't have been an accurate portrayal of how they were entering into their inheritance.

What does He command? He commanded that they take the ark of glory out from behind the veil, and have the priests carry it right into the middle of the Jordan river in <u>full view</u> of the entire congregation. He set it off a certain distance from the congregation where all of them could see the ark as they passed over. The ark in the midst of the river stopped the water from flowing and created a way for the people to enter in.

The way that God describes this plan to the people is very interesting.

> ***Joshua 3:3*** *And they commanded the people, saying, "**When you see the ark** of the covenant of the LORD your God, and the priests, the Levites, bearing it, then you **shall set out from your place and go after it**. Jos 3:4 Yet there shall be a space between you and it, about two thousand cubits by measure. Do not come near it, **that you may know the way by which you must go, for you have not passed this way before**."*

Now keep in mind that this river is not very big. It averages only about 17 to 25 yards across in most places. It is nothing like the Red Sea, or even the Nile or Mississippi River. It's not like they couldn't see across or have easily found their way to the other side. But listen to the language here - "When you see the ark, go out from your place after it. And then you will know the way because you have not passed this way before."

This is such strange language. It almost sounds like they are passing into a pitch black cave and the ark of the covenant is the only lamp that they have. It sounds like there was no possible way for them to find their way across this little river unless the ark created that way and pointed to exactly where and how they could cross.

That is exactly what I'm trying to describe about sanctification. The way out of one country, kindred, and father's house, and the way into another is guarded by the Jordan River. It is guarded by a wall that can only be crossed by faith. The inheritance that God has given to you and set apart for you when you came out from Egypt is accessed when you begin to see the glory of the Lord. **Only in seeing the Lord can you pass into an experience of your inheritance. Only when you see the Lord can you "set out from your place and go after it." Because until you begin to see Him by faith, you simply do not know the way. With the natural eye and the natural mind, you have never passed this way before.**

This is where we misunderstand everything. We think that this land can be possessed by sight. We think that we can know Christ in the flesh, that we can inherit Christ's blessings and promises in the earth. We think that our eyes can know Him, and our ears can hear Him, and our mind can perceive the things that God has given. But the Lord tells Joshua that you cannot even set out from the place where you are until you see the ark. You cannot even see the way that you must go until the glory of the Lord appears. When you see Him in this way, it strikes you with such truth and reality that, indeed, despite all of your effort and learning and determination and prayer and fasting, you have never gone this way before. It's a foreign country, a foreign kindred, a foreign father's house. Just as God said to Abraham, it is one that must be SHOWN TO YOU.

This is what I mean when I say that the land is guarded by faith. The inheritance is inaccessible to all natural senses and natural minds. In 1 Corinthians, Paul says something that is often misquoted and misunderstood. He says,

> ***1Corinthians 2:9*** *But as it is written: "Eye has not seen, nor ear heard, nor have entered into the heart of man the things which God has prepared for those who love Him" 10* <u>*But God has revealed them to us through His Spirit*</u>*. For the Spirit searches all things, yes, the deep things of God.*

In the revealing of Christ by the Spirit of God, we can see the inheritance. When we begin to genuinely grow in faith, then we are set apart unto the unseen inheritance of God. Sanctification working in our soul allows us to look not at those things which are seen, but at those which are unseen.

Let's look back to a few verses that we read in the

beginning and see if they are more clear to us now. In these New Testament scriptures we can see the fulfillment of what we just read in Joshua.

> ***John 17:17*** *Sanctify them in Your Truth; Your Word is Truth. 18 As You have sent Me into the world, I also have sent them into the world, 19 and I sanctify Myself for them, that they also may be sanctified in Truth.*

> ***Acts 20:32*** *And now, brothers, I commend you to God and to the Word of His grace, which is able to build up and to give you inheritance among all those being sanctified.*

> ***Acts 26:14*** *And all of us falling to the ground, I heard a voice speaking to me, and saying in the Hebrew dialect, Saul, Saul why do you persecute Me? It is hard for you to kick against the prods. 15 And I said, Who are you, Sir? And He said, I am Jesus whom you persecute; 16 but rise up and stand on your feet, for it is for this reason I appeared to you, to appoint you a servant and a witness both of what you saw, and in what I shall appear to you, 17 having delivered you from the people and the nations, to whom I now send you, 18 to open their eyes, and to turn them from darkness to light, and from the authority of Satan to God, in order that they may receive remission of sins, and an inheritance among those being sanctified by faith in Me.*

2Thessalonians 2:13 *But we ought to thank God always concerning you, brothers, beloved by the Lord, because God chose you from the beginning to salvation in sanctification of the Spirit and faith in the truth, 14 to which He called you through our gospel, to obtain the glory of our Lord Jesus Christ.*

Our Inheritance

I believe we are in a better place now to understand what Peter is describing in the following verse.

1Peter 1:3 *Blessed be the God and Father of our Lord Jesus Christ, Who, according to His great mercy, has regenerated us to a living hope (lit. expectation) through the resurrection of Jesus Christ from the dead, 4 to an inheritance incorruptible and undefiled and unfading, having been kept in Heaven for you 5 the ones in the power of God being guarded through faith to a salvation ready to be revealed in the last time.*

Can you see what Peter is talking about here? We have been regenerated, born again, into a living expectation. In the shadow, Moses would have said, you have been regenerated by the Passover Lamb and left Egypt, and you have come out into a great expectation. There is an inheritance. It is incorruptible, undefiled, and unfading. It's all yours, but it's not in this wilderness. It's completely yours for the possessing. But you won't see it here in the desert. Eyes can see the *provision* in the wilderness. Eyes can see the miracles in the earth, but only faith can see the kingdom beyond the Jordan. Only faith can see God's purpose and glory in the promised land. It's all beyond the Jordan. It is accessed by faith. You can only go there when you're seeing the glory of the Lord. You can only possess it when the ark is showing you the way. There is an inheritance that is kept for you. It's not kept *from* you; it's kept for you. It is entirely heavenly. There is nothing natural about it. There is nothing earthly to your inheritance. It's incorruptible in the heavens.

Do we realize that there is absolutely nothing natural about our inheritance in the Lord? Our inheritance is not our family and friends, or our health and protection. It is certainly not our wealth or provision. Even if God gave you all of the money and power in the world, that would have nothing to do with your inheritance. That's the wrong realm, the wrong man, the wrong treasure. It is not there. Jesus says, "Where your treasure is, there your heart will be also." And that is always our problem.

But there is an inheritance. Peter says it is yours. It is kept FOR you, but it is kept for you *in the heavens*, not in the earth. It is in Christ, not in Adam. Peter describes the way it is accessed - it is known by faith and ready to be revealed.

A Summary

We've talked about how God has divided the first from the second. We've seen how the death of Christ accomplished a judicial end to the first man, the first creation, and the first covenant. God has no relationship with it. If He touches the natural realm now, He touches it only to invite us out from it. Miracles and revivals have this purpose behind them.

In the resurrection and ascension of Jesus Christ, God drew a line between the Himself and the natural universe. The only way for you and I to know God, to come to God, to escape this realm and man, is to be born from above. To be born of a completely different realm. We cross the divide only when the man on one side dies with Christ on the cross, and our souls are made partakers of the Man on the other side.

This is the miracle of new birth, and it is also the *fact* of sanctification - a great division and separation where God judged the world, and yet saved those in the world who would leave the world in His Son, be crucified to it and raised out from it.

Then there is the experience of the soul where the Truth is faced, and the residue of the first is washed away from our hearts. We haven't literally brought the first with us into Christ, but until we see the reality of the second, the first is all that we know. Until we see the reality of Christ, though we are born of the Spirit, we are perfectly ignorant of the life and realm that is spiritual.

In the language of type and shadow, we are then out of Egypt, but not yet in the land. We left Egypt, but has Egypt left us? We are out of the land slavery to sin and death, and yet we can be divided from our inheritance by a veil that still lies over our heart. The Red Sea has parted, but the Jordan River parts only when we see the ark. The Egyptians are dead, struck by the hand of the Lord on the night we left Egypt. But have we begun to see that we also died that night? Have we begun to realize that we died in the Lamb and were passed over by death because we had already been judged?

We stand at the banks of the Jordan River. We are those who have come out, but have had no idea what it means to come in. We are those who have been sanctified from Egypt as a matter of FACT, but we are those who have yet to have the reproach of Egypt rolled away from our hearts as a matter of inward experience. This, the Bible says, happened only in Joshua chapter 5 when they crossed the Jordan River in full view of the glory of God.

We are those who have been sanctified as a matter of fact, but still, we can remain unsanctified as a matter of inward reality, experience, and possession. How does that happen? Where does sanctification begin? It begins at the Jordan River when faith shows us a way that we have not gone before, a way that we could not have known before. It begins at the Jordan where the Lord's people can cross over in view of the glory of God and leave their flesh at the banks of the river.

This land is guarded by faith. The Israelites could not pass into, or even SEE, the land of inheritance until they saw through the eyes of God. **The heavens are opened to us in the resurrection of Jesus Christ, but the heavens are always guarded by faith. When we begin to experience His mind, then we begin to access what only He can see.**

It is in this way that we are sanctified by faith. We forget what is behind and lay hold of what God has laid before us. We heed the upward call of God in Christ. It is in this way that we leave our country, kindred, and father's house and find the inheritance that must be shown to us.

We come out, like Lot, and never look back. Only when we see the ark of glory do we see the way that we have not gone before.

Made in the USA
Charleston, SC
17 March 2015